TYLER
NINJA
BLEVINS

TWITCH'S TOP STREAMER WITH 11 MILLION+ FOLLOWERS

Adam Furgang

rosen publishing's
rosen central

New York

For Caleb—player of Fortnite *and one of Ninja's biggest fans*

Published in 2020 by The Rosen Publishing Group, Inc.
29 East 21st Street, New York, NY 10010

First Edition

Library of Congress Cataloging-in-Publication Data

Names: Furgang, Adam, author.
Title: Tyler "Ninja" Blevins: Twitch's Top Streamer with 11 Million+ Followers / Adam Furgang.
Description: First edition. | New York : Rosen Central, 2020. | Series: Top video gamers in the world | Includes bibliographical references and index. | Audience: Grades 5–8.
Identifiers: LCCN 2018042725| ISBN 9781725346017 (library bound) | ISBN 9781725346000 (pbk.)
Subjects: LCSH: Blevins, Tyler, 1991– —Juvenile literature. | Video gamers—Biography—Juvenile literature.
Classification: LCC GV1469.3.B58 F87 2020 | DDC 794.8092 [B] —dc23
LC record available at https://lccn.loc.gov/2018042725

Manufactured in the United States of America

On the cover: Shown here at his Ninja Vegas '18 event, Tyler Blevins is one of the most successful video gamers of all time.

CONTENTS

INTRODUCTION

One of the most famous—and highest paid—e-sports video game stars in the world is Tyler Blevins. Blevins, known by his online alias, Ninja, is popular for playing the video game *Fortnite*, published by Epic Games. Blevins grew up playing video games, and he has competed in games such as *Halo* and *Destiny*. He truly rose to fame in 2017, when *Fortnite* was released. The most popular version of this free-to-play video game is a specific mode called *Fortnite: Battle Royale*. In this game, as many as 100 players play at once in a free-for-all competition, battling to the death to become the last player or group alive. Blevins started playing *Fortnite* soon after its release, and his skill and popularity rose quickly. By 2018, Blevins had 10.2 million followers on the video game–streaming service Twitch and 16.4 million subscribers on YouTube. Blevins was also the first person in Twitch history to break 10 million followers.

Video game competitions have been popular since before the rise of YouTube and Twitch. Since the very beginnings of the industry in the early 1970s, gamers have played against one another in competitions. The first gaming competition ever held was called the Intergalactic Spacewar Olympics, which took place on October 19, 1972, at Stanford University's Artificial Intelligence Laboratory. There, a group of gamers gathered to play a video game titled *Spacewar*. At the time, reporter Stewart Brand—who also organized and participated in the competition—wrote an article for *Rolling Stone* magazine titled "Fanatic Life and Symbolic Death Among the Computer Bums." According to the *Rolling Stone* article, "Spacewar

Tyler Blevins went from playing video games with his father and older brothers to entertaining millions of followers under his Twitch handle, Ninja.

consists of two humans, two sets of control buttons or joysticks, one TV-like display and one computer. Two spaceships are displayed in motion on the screen, controllable for thrust, yaw, pitch, and the firing of torpedoes. Whenever a spaceship and torpedo meet, they disappear in an attractive explosion."

Since those early days of video games in the 1970s, the industry has been growing steadily. In 2017, the video game industry generated worldwide revenues of $108.4 billion. Video game competitions among professional gamers or celebrities are now referred to as e-sports. Millions of viewers watch and type comments on their screens as professionals are playing their favorite games. The e-sports industry has grown into its own multimillion-dollar business. Streaming video games—which is when someone plays a video game live online—has become its own form of entertainment. According to a Newzoo market report cited in an Amazon App blog by Emily Esposito Fulkerson, e-sports revenue jumped from $493 million in 2016 to $655 million in 2017. Newzoo estimates that global e-sports revenue could exceed $900 million in 2018.

Today, Blevins is one of the highest-paid e-sports stars in the world. He reportedly earns more than $500,000 a month from his Twitch partnership, subscriber donations, YouTube advertising, and sponsors, including the energy drink company Red Bull. Aside from his skills playing *Fortnite*, Blevins is also a very entertaining personality to watch. With his often colorfully dyed hair, Ninja can be found on Twitch commenting as he plays *Fortnite*, sometimes streaming for as many as ten hours a day.

CHAPTER 1

Origins of a Gamer

Before he became one of the most popular and recognizable gamers in the world, Tyler Blevins was just an ordinary kid who had a typical childhood.

Blevins was born on June 5, 1991, in Lake Villa, Illinois, as Richard Tyler Blevins. He grew up in the village of Grayslake in Lake County, Illinois. His parents, Chuck and Cynthia, had two sons before Tyler, named John and Chris.

While Blevins was growing up, his father was a big fan of video games himself. He often brought many new games home when they were released. Blevins credits his father as the main influence behind his love of video games, which led to his lucrative career at such a young age. When Blevins was younger, his father would often bring home Sega Genesis games for him and his brothers to play. Though all three siblings had early bedtimes, their father would often stay up playing video games after they went to bed—sometimes until well past midnight.

In November 2001, *Halo: Combat Evolved*, a futuristic multiplayer war game, was launched on Microsoft's Xbox gaming console. The game was an instant success. Blevins was ten years old at the time, and he often had to watch, frustrated, while his older brothers played *Halo* without him. They felt he was too young to join in. Once given the chance, "he just destroyed us," his brother John

One of the games Blevins played when he was a child was the Xbox exclusive science fiction first-person shooter *Halo: Combat Evolved*. He would later go on to play *Halo* competitively.

admitted in a CNBC.com article by Ali Montag. His brother Chris said, "He would stay up past the wee hours and just keep working. I think that's when we were like, 'Okay, maybe we're not going to play with Tyler anymore.'"

In a 2015 interview with YouTube personality Walshy, Blevins recalled playing various video games from his childhood, "There was this incredible Jurassic Park game that was for the Sega Genesis that was incredible. It was weird: You could be the raptor or the human … It was weird, man. It was the coolest video game ever."

He also fondly remembered playing a Power Rangers video game and said, "I basically played every single game you can imagine, like all the time, all day, on the Sega Genesis. Then, moving forward, I believe the first FPS [first-person shooter] I played was, ah, *Perfect Dark* … We didn't own it, though."

Blevins explained to Walshy that his mother did not like violent video games and would monitor all new games that came into the home. As a result, Blevins often went to friends' homes to play games he was not allowed to play at home. Despite the restrictions on the games brought into the house, his father continued to purchase

A Video Game Creation Story

Humans have been playing games for thousands of years. The oldest dice discovered date back as far as seven thousand to eight thousand years ago.

Physicist William Higinbotham created the first video game, titled *Tennis for Two*, on October 18, 1958, at the Brookhaven National Laboratory. Similar to the classic *Pong* video game from the 1970s, Higinbotham's game was a simplified version of tennis. Many people enjoyed playing *Tennis for Two* with separate controllers that allowed for competition.

The first home video game system was called the Magnavox Odyssey. Ralph Baer developed the system while working at Sanders Associates, Inc., in the 1960s. He eventually sold the license to Magnavox in 1972. Magnavox mass-produced the system for several years.

The most famous of all early video game consoles was the Atari 2600. The Atari 2600 was released in 1977 and went on to sell more than thirty million consoles. On April 2, 2016, the National Video Game Museum opened in Frisco, Texas. The Atari 2600, along with many other gaming consoles that followed, can be seen on display there.

all the latest Xbox and PlayStation consoles, and Tyler and his brothers became avid video game players.

Not All Fun and Games

Blevins attended Grayslake North High School in Grayslake, Illinois, from 2005 until 2009. While still being a passionate player of video games, he excelled as a student in high school and even found time to play soccer and held a part-time job for three years at the casual restaurant chain Noodles & Company.

In Ali Montag's CNBC.com article, Blevins explained how he convinced his parents to allow him to play video games as a career:

> I maintained my job that I was working at Noodles and Company, and I stayed in college while I was doing all these things. I continued to do well in school and focus on, like, the future of my life, as well as working on streaming and competing in *Halo*. It was one of those things where, like, if I was doing well in school, putting in the time and effort there, in soccer as well, that I would be rewarded to play as many games as I want.

Microsoft's Xbox and Sony's PlayStation are the two biggest consoles used in competitive gaming.

Blevins went on to say that he encourages his fans—many of whom also hope to turn gaming into a job—not to drop everything just to play video games.

In addition to schoolwork, sports, and gaming, Blevins continued working throughout high school and into college. He first started competing with games playing the Xbox game *Halo* in 2009. After high school, he attended Silver Lake College from 2009 until 2010. It was at

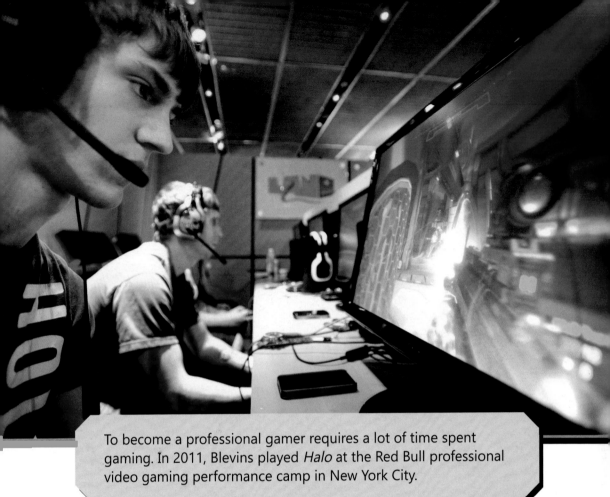

To become a professional gamer requires a lot of time spent gaming. In 2011, Blevins played *Halo* at the Red Bull professional video gaming performance camp in New York City.

this time that Blevins decided to pursue his career in gaming full time, and he dropped out.

Gaming Runs in the Family

Playing games definitely runs in the Blevins family. In February 2015, Tyler Blevins's family appeared on three episodes of the TV game show *Family Feud*. Typically, a family needs to audition in person to get a chance to play *Family Feud*. Because there were no audition locations near their home, it was Tyler's idea to make an audition video instead. The creative effort to get his family onto the famous game show paid off—after making and submitting the video, Tyler and his two older brothers, Chris and John, were asked to audition in person. They were then accepted to appear on the show. They appeared along with Johnathan's wife, Jodi, and her brother-in-law, Cody Meetz. At the time, Chris Blevins was working as a substitute teacher at Grayslake North High School and many of his students tuned in to watch the episodes of the show. Over the course of the three episodes they appeared in, the Blevins family won $41,000.

CHAPTER 2

Game Time!

Much like traditional athletic sports, e-sports involves professional game players or teams competing against one another in sports arenas, with the games broadcast on large video screens. Successful e-sports stars might be paid through sponsors (for example, by the company that makes their preferred brand of controller), and many competitive tournaments award money for winning. This new and quickly growing business is estimated to be valued at $1.5 billion by 2020, according to a report by Peter Warman of Newzoo. According to Ana Valens on dotesports.com, "more people watch online gaming videos than HBO, Netflix, ESPN, and Hulu all combined together."

Fans of e-sports can watch gaming competitions online on various video-streaming services, the most popular being Twitch and YouTube. Streaming is an exciting way to watch people play games because everything is happening live, with little editing involved. Streaming is not just limited to e-sports—it is the technology used to watch, rent, or buy movies and television shows online. It can also be used to send or receive video calls.

There are many other e-sports streaming services, such as instagib.tv, smashcast.tv, mixer.com, and steampowered.com. On many of these sites, viewers can watch live or previously recorded games, interviews, or industry news reports.

As competitive professional leagues and tournaments reach final playoffs or final seasons, games are held in huge venues with very large, arena-style screens that display the games for live spectators in addition to being streamed over the internet. Often, the winning prizes at these large tournaments are in the thousands—or even millions—of dollars.

E-sports have become a new billion-dollar industry. Shown here is a live match during the International 2018 *DotA 2* Championships at Rogers Arena in Vancouver, Canada.

Blevins Takes the Stage

Blevins began seriously playing competitive video games when he realized that he could win a lot in prize money. According to Ali Montag of CNBC.com, he stated, "I started realizing, 'Oh my God, you can actually go to these events, I can actually make a team and I can compete against them," he says. "That was when stuff got real."

His first professional appearance was in Orlando, Florida, in 2009, in a *Halo 3* competition. He continued playing over the years and joined established teams, including Team Liquid and Renegades. In 2012, he was on a team that won a *Halo 4* competition.

Blevins's father noticed the gradual improvement in his son's online gaming success. "You know you argue with him about how much time he's spending on it, and he starts making a little money here and there, and it's nothing. Then the next thing you know, he tells me 'I'm getting streams. I'm getting subscriptions. I'm getting sponsors.' And I'm thinking, 'Where is this coming from?'"

Blevins explained that the hard work was necessary for his success. "You have to be better than hundreds of people, thousands of people—you have to be the best player to even win money from tournaments."

Breaking into the *Fortnite* Mainstream

After competing with other games, Tyler Blevins gained worldwide fame when he started dedicating his efforts to only playing and streaming his *Fortnite* games on Twitch.

Fortnite: Battle Royale was created by Epic Games and released for free on PC, Xbox One, and PlayStation 4 on September 26, 2017. The game makes money by selling additional cosmetic skins, which are virtual—and often colorful—costumes, to players through an in-game store. Despite the fact that *Fortnite* is free to download, as of July, 2018, in-game purchases have earned the game as much as $1 billion, with no signs of slowing.

According to an article by Hayley Tsukayama in the *Washington Post*, "*Fortnite* has been described as a cross between *Minecraft* and a shooter game. Survival is the name of the game. Players fight each other, making it through a night of zombies, or surviving to the end of a massive battle, and they use the landscape around them to find materials to build shelters."

According to industry analyst Mat Piscatella in an article by the *Washington Posts's* Hayley Tsukayama, *Fortnite* is "not just

Blevins often pairs up with other professional gamers. In 2011, Ninja and David "Walshy" Walsh played competitive *Halo* together.

Pairing Up with DrLupo

In *Fortnite: Battle Royale*, people can form teams with up to four players. Tyler Blevins frequently teams up with another famous gamer, Ben Lupo, who goes by the online alias DrLupo.

Lupo created his Twitch account in 2013 while playing the video game *Diablo*. He then went on to invest more than seven thousand hours playing the Bungie first-person shooter *Destiny*. After improving his skills in the game, he started to charge people to help them play the game.

After *Destiny*, DrLupo went on to play a video game called *Playerunknown's Battlegrounds (PUBG)*, where he met Blevins. Ninja and DrLupo's friendship began there, and the two helped one another to gain more and more Twitch followers. They have even met up in the real world. According to Lupo, "My father passed away this past March ... The first person to be at the airport was Ninja—he was one of the first people I told since it felt like everything was falling down around me."

DrLupo has more than 2.1 million followers on Twitch and close to 1 million subscribers on YouTube.

the biggest game of the year, it's the first game we've seen since *Minecraft* that's had this kind of appeal."

From *Game Jam* to *Fortnite*

Darren Sugg is the game developer and designer of the popular game *Fortnite*, but he did not come up with the idea for the smash hit alone. *Fortnite* started during a game jam at Epic Games. A game jam is similar to a musical jam session, when musicians get

The popular 2017 video game *Fortnite* was developed by Epic Games. Blevins shot to fame by playing *Fortnite* on Twitch.

together to improvise and create new music. In a game jam, game designers gather to conceptualize as many new games as possible in a short period of time.

According to a Polygon.com article by Michael McWhertor, Epic Games CEO and founder Tim Sweeney said, "It [*Fortnite*] started out as an internal game jam project at Epic and has grown over time. We have a combination of a great building game, an action-combat game and with some elements of an MMO."

Sugg described his idea for the game in an interview with allgamers.com, describing it as "a cooperative action building game, where players loot, craft, and defend forts against hordes of creatures all in a procedurally generated world. In short, make Weapons, make Forts and make Friends."

It is important to note that the *Battle Royale* portion of *Fortnite* is just a single game mode within the game as a whole—but it is by far the most popular and best known.

From Home Gamer to World Stardom

Throughout his years at Grayslake North High School, from 2005 until 2009, Tyler Blevins was no stranger to traditional sports. Blevins played on his school's varsity soccer team, the Knights. Blevins and his brothers were also big fans of the National Football League team the Detroit Lions.

For a time, Blevins was not sure if he would pursue a career in pro soccer or pro e-sports. Having always played video games, too, it was his parents who requested he make a choice. During high school, Blevins learned about MLG (Major League Gaming), which has been one of the leading forces in competitive video gaming since the early 2000s.

In a 2011 interview with John Gaudiosi in *Forbes*, Blevins described this decision:

> I always played video games my entire life. It was my parents who told me to make a choice: *Are you going to continue to play video games or are you going to go with soccer?* I found out about MLG and I decided to go into video games. That was my junior year and I still played soccer my whole high school career, but I definitely started to put more time and effort into video games.

Major League Gaming is one of the most recognizable names in the professional video gaming world. Their competitions draw thousands of fans to watch the teams compete.

In 2009, Blevins played in a competition for the first time in a *Halo 3* MLG event in Orlando, Florida. After finishing high school, Blevins enrolled at Silver Lake College and continued working at Noodles & Company. Because his gaming career was heating up in 2010, he dropped out of Silver Lake College after just one year. What video game was Blevins focused on at the time? The Xbox game *Halo: Reach*.

Around the same time, streaming was just beginning to gain widespread popularity, and Blevins was one of the very first to play *Halo* and stream his gameplay from his basement in Illinois. At the time, Blevins was making about $100 a day streaming from Twitch. Blevins described a typical day in his interview with Gaudiosi when he stated:

I'll wake up. I'll maybe get some breakfast, walk downstairs in my basement and just turn everything on and start streaming my gameplay for about ten hours. I make money off of ads that Justin.TV and Twitch.TV allow me to use through their partnership. I'll take a couple of breaks for some food, but other than that, that's pretty much all I do is play video games and practice with my team.

In 2011, Blevins went on to compete in the MLG National Championships, which were held in Providence, Rhode Island. Blevins competed playing *Halo: Reach* for Team Turning Point. He began traveling and continued to play *Halo: Reach* and other games competitively at tournaments in Texas, Ohio, and California. By 2012, Blevins's team won the *Halo 4* MLG Fall Championships. Blevins took the distinction of having the highest score in the final game.

Blevins's Eye Operation

In 2014, as his streaming career was beginning to take off, Blevins began experiencing headaches around his right eye. He went to his doctor and learned that there was a problem with his retina. The retina is the layer at the back of the eye that contains light-sensitive cells. This part of the eye sends and receives messages to and from the brain to help form a visual image. His doctor told him that

Ninja has become Tyler Blevins's professional brand and nickname. Blevins is seen here reacting to his logo being displayed at the Ninja Vegas '18 event at the E-Sports Arena in Las Vegas.

Embracing the Ninja

On Twitch, YouTube, and elsewhere in the gaming world, *Fortnite* fans know Tyler Blevins by his online alias: Ninja. How did he come to get this iconic nickname? Before he became famous for playing *Fortnite*, Blevins made a name for himself playing games in the *Halo* franchise, and this is where he got his now-famous online name. Blevins explained to TooFab.com why he calls himself Ninja:

> So there's like a little move back in the *Halo* days whenever you were getting chased if you went around a corner, and the guy followed you and you jumped over his head and like backsmacked him. It was called like, *the ninja*. So, when I did [that move], I was like, "ah man ... I want to make that my name."

After performing the *Halo* ninja move again and again, Blevins used the name and it stuck. Now, after shooting to the top of the video game world, millions of people recognize the name Ninja.

he had retinal defects, which had caused the retina to become detached. Scarring was occurring as a result. It is not known what caused the condition, but Blevins was told that he was very lucky that he had not already gone blind in that eye. Having an eye issue is a major scare for any professional gamer because gamers' jobs involve looking at a screen for hours at a time. Blevins knew he would have to address this problem before it got any worse and his gaming career was ruined.

On August 15, 2014, Blevins announced on his YouTube channel that he was going in for eye surgery and that he would not be able to game for two weeks afterward.

After the surgery, however, Blevins realized he had been too optimistic. Despite the two-week timeline he made for himself, his healing process took longer than expected—and he could not play video games or stream for months. This was a difficult problem for the popular e-sports star, as he was used to streaming for up to ten hours a day. Confined to his bed for months, his Twitch streams dropped from 4,500 viewers to as few as 400. An extremely popular new game—*Destiny*—launched September 9, 2014, but Blevins was still unable to play. This was a huge missed opportunity for him to gain new fans by playing the newest, most popular title at the time. He made another YouTube announcement on September 17, 2014, that he would likely not be back for a few more weeks so his eye could heal more.

Blevins was unable to get right back into gaming because of how damaging it can be over long periods of time. The rapid eye movement that occurs during gaming was not good for the healing process. Taking care of one's eyesight is important for everyone, but especially for gamers, who stare at video monitors for many hours a day. Taking breaks is an important part of gaming, both for professionals and amateurs.

The wounds from Blevins's surgery eventually healed, and he was able to return to video game streaming. He regained his Twitch following, and within a few years, he acquired more than ten million followers.

Jessica Goch

Along with his career in video gaming, another important piece of Tyler Blevins's life is his wife, Jessica. She was born Jessica Goch on June 23, 1992, in Schofield, Wisconsin. Jessica attended Wausau West High School in Wausau, Wisconsin, and performed on the varsity dance team. After high school, she went on to study interpersonal communication and human resource management at the University of Wisconsin–Whitewater.

Jessica Goch and Tyler Blevins first met at a *Focus Fire Halo* Tournament in La Crosse, Wisconsin, in 2010. Like Blevins, Jessica was involved in gaming and she had loved video games since childhood. Her online alias is JGhosty.

Blevins once explained to fans in a YouTube video how he almost did not go to the tournament where he met Jessica because of an impending snowstorm. He braved the weather, however, and at the tournament he met Goch for the first time. Blevins had a girlfriend at the time, so they did not date immediately, but the two kept in touch over social media and they started dating about a year later.

After dating for several years, Goch and Blevins got engaged to be married on November 22, 2016. It was announced on Ninja's Twitter account with the tweet, "Boys … she said yes!! Engaged to @JGh0sty." They were married on August 8, 2017, at the Lehmann Mansion in Lake Villa, Illinois. Their wedding video can be seen on YouTube. The day after they were married, Blevins announced the news on YouTube and let fans know that they would be honeymooning in Germany, where he would be competing in a *PUBG (PlayerUnknown's Battlegrounds)* tournament in Cologne. Blevins also announced that he would be broadcasting more than four days of recent Twitch streams on his Twitch site while he was away so his fans would have something to watch.

Working as his manager, Jessica "JGhosty" Blevins introduces her husband, Tyler "Ninja" Blevins, at Ninja Vegas '18.

After their one-year wedding anniversary, Jessica posted on Twitter, "My heart is so full. One year of marriage, six years of dating, and eight years of knowing each other. ❤ ❤ @Ninja".

Today, Jessica serves as Tyler Blevins's manager and accompanies him to tournaments and gaming events. Jessica also has her own Twitch channel, JGhosty, with more than 325,000 followers and more than 1.4 million views. She is also on various social media sites, where she posts about video games, her personal life, and, of course, Ninja.

CHAPTER 4

Making It Big in Gaming

The rising popularity of video game–streaming has paralleled the extreme success of the video game streaming website Twitch. As interest in video games—among both old and young gamers—across the world increased, Twitch became the platform for its success. Instead of just playing a game, people were more and more interested in watching someone else play.

Now the world's most popular streaming website, Twitch was founded and created by Justin Kan. Streaming video games was not Kan's initial idea for a site. Kan started with Justin.tv, a social "lifestreaming" video site, in 2005. Lifestreaming, or lifecasting, is the practice of broadcasting much of one's entire life—live— on the internet. At the time, Kan was studying at Yale University and working toward a degree in physics and psychology.

Twitch has become the biggest source for all things streaming—especially in video games—and anyone can sign up for an account online and stream their gameplay live.

MAKING IT BIG IN GAMING

Internet Safety

Playing video games online, participating in chat groups, or streaming gameplay live for all to see can be an exciting and fun way to socialize and interact with friends. It is possible to meet new people and even make friends through video games and various gaming platforms. While this is all exciting, it is also important to stay safe online. Some people take advantage of anyone who shares too much personal information online, which can be dangerous.

- Always be polite and respectful with anything posted or said. Anything posted on the internet is permanent, so be careful about what you write.

- Get a parent's permission to play with strangers online.

- Never use your full name with strangers online.

- Never give your passwords, home address, or any personal information out to anyone.

- Use a strong password that has a combination of uppercase and lowercase letters, numbers, and symbols. For example, AaXx1@*8 has numbers, symbols, and both capital and lowercase letters.

- Never use the same password twice. There are random password generators available online, and they can help you keep track of your unique passwords as well.

Explosive Success: Switching to Twitch

In 2007, the Justin.tv site officially launched and Justin Kan's life was streamed on its homepage. According to Kevin Morris at dailydot.com, "Viewers watched Kan from his point of view, joining him as he ate his breakfast, walked down the street, worked at his laptop, and—as the gimmick of the experiment started to draw national media attention—appeared on morning television shows such as the *Today Show*."

Accounting for this enormous success was easy: Streaming video—no matter the topic—was an interesting new way to produce content. As webcams and computer-related products dropped in cost around this same time, access to streaming technology was quick and easy. Before the focus switched to video gaming, livestreaming everyday activities drove the Justin.tv platform forward. Innovators soon came up with news ideas for making entertaining live videos, and so Twitch was born.

Twitch grew out of Justin.tv as a video-streaming service in 2011. By 2014, Twitch had become so popular that Justin.tv renamed itself Twitch Interactive and the original Justin.tv was shut down for good.

Tyler Blevins first started streaming on Justin.tv in 2011 and quickly switched to Twitch when the service became available. Soon after Twitch split into its own service, rumors spread that Google might buy Twitch for as much as $1 billion. Then, in August 2014, the online retail giant Amazon announced it would be buying the video game streaming service for $970 million. This marked the start of a new era for video gamers.

Making Money on Twitch

According to Ali Montag of CNBC.com, Blevins earns around $500,000 a month on Twitch streaming his *Fortnite* gameplay. That is a huge amount, but how does he do it? The short answer is simple: advertising. The long answer is because Ninja is very

The online retail giant Amazon purchased Twitch in 2014. A Twitch membership is now included as part of Amazon's paid premium service, Amazon Prime.

good at playing video games, he's entertaining to watch, and he streams a lot.

Before his huge success, Blevins started out just like everyone else on Twitch. As his popularity grew, he received a payment each week, which was made up of advertising money (some of which gets shared with Twitch). Makers of video games and other products pay Twitch to feature their games or products on the website. Users on Twitch can customize their streams on their broadcast dashboards and determine how many ads will play during a livestream. The ads appear onscreen, similar to the way advertisements on traditional

TV shows are placed throughout a broadcast. Successful streamers, like Ninja, get paid the most because they have more viewers on their pages clicking on the advertisements they see.

Another way to make money through Twitch is with sponsors. When a gamer's e-sports stream is popular, brands take notice and will sometimes offer a streamer free products—or even pay the streamer to help them promote their brand. One of the brands Tyler Blevins is sponsored by is the energy drink Red Bull. People watching Ninja's Twitch stream might see a small refrigerator behind him stocked with Red Bull. This is a paid promotion from the energy drink company.

Popular streamers on Twitch can also get donations from fans to help fund their streaming. Tyler Blevins once received a Twitch donation for $62,000 from a single user in one day.

With a large enough following, a Twitch user can become part of the Twitch Partner Program. This program gives popular Twitch users even more of an opportunity to make money in the form of paid subscribers to a channel. For a small fee, users get access to special features, including chats and past video archives of a streamer. Twitch has more than 2 million streamers, but only about 1.5 percent are part of the Partner Program, according to the site's FAQ. Subscribing to Blevins's stream, for example, allows users to comment and sometimes even get a response from Ninja himself.

CHAPTER 5

The Future for Ninja

One of the greatest keys to Ninja's success is staying popular and keeping his fans happy. Sometimes that means attracting celebrity attention to his livestreams. For example, on March 15, 2018, music star Drake started playing *Fortnite* with Blevins on Twitch. Professional football player JuJu Smith-Schuster of the Pittsburgh Steelers and rapper Travis Scott also joined to complete the four-man team. Word about the match quickly spread, and the stream gained more than six hundred thousand viewers. This broke the previous record for most-watched stream in Twitch history by more than two hundred thousand viewers.

Ninja Vegas '18

In addition to a busy streaming schedule, Blevins still attends gaming competitions and tournaments In April 2018, Ninja competed in a gaming event he created called Ninja Vegas '18. The event was held in the Esports Arena at the Luxor Hotel in Las Vegas, Nevada. Ninja competed against fans for $50,000 in prize money for fans who could kill him in a round of *Fortnite*. The entire event was streamed live on Twitch.

For every round Blevins won, he donated $2,500 to the Alzheimer's Association. If a player managed to defeat Ninja during a round,

Tyler Blevins has become a recognized celebrity, even outside the world of games. At live e-sports events, he often dyes his hair different colors and dresses in his Ninja logo colors: bright yellow or blue.

he or she would get to keep the $2,500. Ninja and his competitors played nine matches throughout the event, and viewership peaked at 660,000—a number that broke his own previous record. After the event on April 22, 2018, Ninja tweeted: "What an incredible event last night. I'll never forget it and the people I met."

Epic's First E3 Celebrity Pro-Am

During one of the gaming industry's annual gaming conventions (the Electronic Entertainment Expo, or E3), Epic Games held its first celebrity event: the *Fortnite* Pro-Am. This huge event was held on July 10, 2018, in the Banc of California Stadium in Los Angeles, California. The event was a great success and attracted more than 1.1 million viewers live on Twitch.

At the event, Blevins paired up with musician DJ Marshmello, who appeared in costume. The *Fortnite* Pro-Am matched celebrities with pro gamers for a $1 million prize to be donated to a charity of their choice. Ninja and Marshmello won matches against fifty other teams. Blevins donated his winnings to the Alzheimer's Association.

Tyler Blevins talks to Christopher Comstock, also known by his online nickname, Marshmello. Ninja and Marshmello won the *Fortnite: Battle Royale* competition at the 2018 E3 convention.

GuardianCon 2018

Blevins was part of another charity event called GuardianCon 2018, which took place in Tampa, Florida. This two-day convention is rooted in both video games and charity, much as Blevins's career has been. The event is organized to raise money for St. Jude Children's Research Hospital through donations and livestreaming popular games. Blevins has been involved in the annual event and streamed for four hours on July 12, 2018, on the GuardianCon Twitch channel. Blevins had various goals and incentives set out so he

The Female Gamer Controversy

With all his fame and popularity, Tyler Blevins has also faced his share of controversy. In August 2018, Blevins revealed to gaming website Polygon.com that he will not stream with female gaming partners because he feels it promotes an atmosphere of bullying and online harassment from viewers.

Blevins also believes that streaming with female gamers will hurt his relationship with his wife. He described this opinion to Polygon: "If I have one conversation with one female streamer where we're playing with one another, and even if there's a hint of flirting, that is going to be taken and going to be put on every single video and be clickbait forever."

Despite claiming that his decision was made out of respect for his wife, gaming media outlets have criticized the Twitch star. Many have argued that this choice is unfair to female streamers. To respond to this controversy, Blevins made a follow-up statement on his Twitter account on August 13, 2018:

While I understand some people have implied my views mean I have something against playing with women, I want to make clear the issue I'm addressing is online harassment, and my attempt to minimize it from our life. It is something that affects all streamers, especially ones that make their relationships public. I wanted to bring attention to this issue and my comments should not be characterized as anything beyond that.

Ninja and his wife know female gamers often face harassment online. Ninja has decided not to stream games with female gamers to help prevent this.

could help the event hit the overall donation goal of $2.7 million. In addition to Blevins, the collective art company Design By Humans and Ninja's frequent gaming partner DrLupo were involved in the charity event to help raise money for the hospital. Design By Humans sold T-shirts with graphic art of Ninja and DrLupo to help raise money for the event.

On the morning of the event, Ninja tweeted, "Sorry I got this up so late! My donation Incentives for the @GuardianCon @StJudeCharity final block today!"

Accompanying his tweet was a list that included Ninja dying his hair, getting tattoos, and streaming while in a cosplay costume if certain charity goals were achieved. For individuals who donated smaller amounts, Ninja pledged to drop his weapons or all his items while playing *Fortnite* to make the game more interesting. With help from Ninja, the charity event achieved its goal and raised $2.7 million.

Career Advice from Ninja

There are many difficulties that go along with working as a professional video gamer. Whether streaming or competing in e-sports tournaments, these gamers dedicate their lives to their craft. They must spend hours every day practicing and staying up to date with the most popular games. Becoming a Twitch star is even harder—it is not enough to just be a skilled player, a streamer must also have an attractive personality. Plenty of people are excellent at video games—but not everyone can consistently make people enjoy the content they create.

A Career in Gaming

The idea of getting paid to play video games for a living like Tyler Blevins is very appealing to a lot of people. However, it is not easy to accomplish. To make money gaming, someone must be extremely skilled at a current and popular game. Even superstar Tyler Blevins did not just start getting paid overnight. He worked hard at it for years, all while going to school, getting good grades, playing soccer, and working at an after-school job. It is important to keep time playing video games balanced with other things in life, such as schoolwork, other activities, and friends and family.

Gaming can be costly, too. Most gamers who play on Twitch have expensive gaming computers. They do not often use home consoles, such as Xbox or PlayStation. A good camera for face streaming, a quality microphone for audio, and a dedicated room to game in are also necessary for a successful stream. These costs can quickly add up.

While game streaming is not a good career choice for everyone, there are plenty of other occupations in the industry. Game designers, writers, programmers, artists, and commentators all contribute to the gaming field. A part-time after-school job at a video game store can also be a fun way to earn money while staying involved with gaming.

Becoming a professional e-sports star is challenging. There are many other careers for people who love video games, such as game developers, writers, designers, artists, and programmers.

The best advice for anyone who wants to one day be a professional video gamer comes from Blevins himself. In an interview with *Forbes* magazine's Paul Tassi, he addressed the idea that so many young people want to succeed as a "YouTube sensation." He stated,

It is very difficult to "make it" as a top broadcaster or YouTuber. I encourage every person to follow their dreams and believe that they can do anything, but the harsh reality is … reality. People need to be true to themselves, and if entertaining and content creating is something that does not come naturally and is really difficult, they should find something they are passionate about and love and do that instead. For me, the only difficulties that I ran into had to be the game that I chose to create content for. I started in *Halo: Reach* and that was the downswing of *Halo*. Less people playing equaled less viewers, and a lower ceiling for my growth. My advice to content creators [gamers] in the future is try to have the foresight to see a popular game coming out, and be the first to make content.

Even with all the challenges that go along with streaming as a full-time job, there is no question that Blevins has become one of the most successful video gamers of all time. Starting young, improving his skills, and having a fun-loving personality have all contributed to his achievements, and any potential future stars would be smart to take his advice to try to follow in his footsteps.

Timeline

1991   Tyler Blevins is born Richard Tyler Blevins in Lake Villa, Illinois.

1992   Jessica Goch is born in Schofield, Wisconsin.

2009   Blevins graduates from Grayslake North High School in Grayslake, Illinois. Blevins competes professionally for the first time, playing *Halo 3* in MLG Orlando.

2010   Blevins decides to pursue his career in gaming full time and drops out of Silver Lake College.
Blevins meets Jessica Goch at a Focus Fire *Halo* Tournament in La Crosse, Wisconsin.

2011   Blevins competes in the MLG National Championships in Providence, Rhode Island.

2014   Blevins has eye surgery for a detached retina.

2015   Blevins's family appears on three episodes of the TV game show *Family Feud*.

2016   Blevins and Goch get engaged.

2017   Goch and Blevins are married on August 8 at Lehmann Mansion in Lake Villa, Illinois.

2018   Rap star Drake starts playing *Fortnite* with Blevins on Twitch, and the stream gains more than six hundred thousand viewers.
Epic Games announces it will supply $100 million to fund the prize pools for tournaments for *Fortnite* during its first year of competitions.
Epic Games holds its first E3 celebrity event, the *Fortnite* Pro-Am, in the Banc of California Stadium, in Los Angeles, California.

GLOSSARY

alias An alternate name, such as one used by an online gamer.

alphanumeric password A password combination made of uppercase and lowercase letters, numbers, and symbols, which is considered safer than passwords without these combinations.

broadband Transmission technique using many frequencies to deliver many messages at the same time.

clickbait Online content designed to encourage viewers to click on a link.

console A specialized computer system designed for playing video games; e.g., PlayStation or Xbox.

corporate sponsor A source of advertising in which a company provides money to a person or event.

dashboard A tool on a website or app that allows the user to view data that is continually updated.

e-sports Competitive video gaming, typically streamed online.

first-person shooter (FPS) Video games played from the point of view of the game character.

free-to-play video game An online game that does not charge the user to play. It makes money from advertisements or sales within the game.

Justin.tv A social lifestreaming video site launched in 2005 by Justin Kan, which later became the video-streaming site Twitch.

lifecasting The practice of broadcasting much of one's life live onto the internet.

millennials People born after 1980, who entered the adult world around the year 2000.

pro-am An event in which professionals and amateurs participate side by side, commonly to raise money for charity.

retina The layer at the back of the eye that contains light-sensitive cells. It can become damaged by looking at screens for too long.

revenue Earnings or profit.

streaming A form of data transmission that allows viewers to watch media content as it is being created.

Twitch Interactive A video-streaming site where many e-sports and competitive gaming streams are hosted.

webcam A camera that connects to the internet so images can be viewed by online viewers.

For More Information

Canada Safety Council

1020 Thomas Spratt Place
Ottawa, ON K1G5L5
Canada
(613) 739-1535
Website: http://canadasafetycouncil.org
Facebook: @canada.safety
Twitter: @CanadaSafetyCSC
The Canada Safety Council provides support and tips for staying
safe online.

Extra Life

c/o Children's Miracle Network Hospitals
205 West 700 South
Salt Lake City, UT 84101
Website: http://www.extra-life.org
Instagram and Twitter: @extraLife4Kids
Extra Life uses online gaming to support users' local Children's
Miracle Network Hospitals, raising money for sick and
injured children.

Federal Trade Commission

600 Pennsylvania Avenue NW
Washington, DC 20580
Website: http://www.consumer.ftc.gov
Facebook: @federaltradecommission
Twitter: @FTC

The FTC has consumer information about online safety, privacy, identity, and online security.

Gamers Outreach

PO Box 694

Saline, MI 48176

Website: http://www.gamersoutreach.org

Facebook, Instagram, and Twitter: @GamersOutreach

Gamers Outreach is a charity organization that provides gaming equipment and experiences to children in hospitals.

World Gaming Network

1303 Yonge Street

Toronto, ON M4T2Y9

Canada

Website: http://www.worldgaming.com

Facebook and Twitter: @WorldGaming

Instagram: @officialworldgaming

The World Gaming Network offers daily competitive e-sports tournaments for players of every skill level.

Andrejkovics, Zoltan. *The Invisible Game: Mindset of a Winning Team*. Seattle, WA: CreateSpace, 2016.

Flanagan, Noob. *Make Money Gaming: How to Earn Money From Live-Streaming Video Games*. Seattle, WA: CreateSpace, 2017.

Hansen, Dustin. *Game On! Video Game History from Pong and Pac-Man to Mario, Minecraft, and More*. New York, NY: Feiwel & Friends, 2016.

Hennessey, Jonathan. *The Comic Book Story of Video Games: The Incredible History of the Electronic Gaming Revolution*. New York, NY: Ten Speed Press, 2017.

Jankowski, Matthew. *The Modern Nerd's Guide to Esports* (Geek Out!). New York, NY: Gareth Stevens Publishing, 2018.

Li, Roland. *Good Luck, Have Fun: The Rise of Esports*. New York, NY: Skyhorse Publishing, 2016.

Parkin, Simon. *An Illustrated History of 151 Video Games*. London, UK: Lorenz Books, 2014.

Prima Games. *Twitch: Creating, Growing & Monetizing Your Livestream*. Roseville, CA: Prima Games, 2019.

Rodriguez, Hector, and Matt Haag, Seth Abner, Will Johnson, et al. *OpTic Gaming: The Making of Esports Champions*. New York, NY: Dey Street Books, 2016.

Snyder, David. *Speedrunning: Interviews with the Quickest Gamers* (Studies in Gaming). Jefferson, NC: McFarland, 2017.

Stubbs, Mike. *Esports: The Ultimate Gamer's Guide*. London, UK: Templar Publishing, 2018.

Taylor, T. L. *Raising the Stakes: E-Sports and the Professionalization of Computer Gaming*. Cambridge, MA: MIT Press, 2015.

BIBLIOGRAPHY

Baker, Chris. "Stewart Brand Recalls First 'Spacewar' Video Game Tournament." *Rolling Stone*, May 25, 2016. https://www .rollingstone.com/culture/culture-news/stewart-brand-recalls -first-spacewar-video-game-tournament-187669.

Farner, Shawn. "The Untold Truth of Tyler 'Ninja' Blevins." Svg.com. Retrieved August 29, 2018. https://www.svg.com/115974/untold -truth-tyler-ninja-blevins.

Fulkerson, Emily Esposito. "Free Download: 2018 Global Esports Market Report by Newzoo." Amazon Appstore Blogs, March 1, 2018. https://developer.amazon.com/fr/blogs/appstore/post /c3558e44-e83a-4c1f-9725-95a013e75889/free-download-2018 -global-esports-market-report-by-newzoo.

Gaudiosi, John. "Pro Gamer Tyler 'Ninja' Blevins Discusses Meteoric Rise of Major League Gaming." *Forbes*, December 6, 2011. https://www.forbes.com/sites/johngaudiosi/2011/12/06 /pro-gamer-tyler-ninja-blevins-discusses-meteoric-rise-of-major -league-gaming/#35225179ea38.

McWhertor, Michael. "What's the Future of Games at Epic Games?" Polygon, March 26, 2014. https://www.polygon .com/2014/3/26/5542822/the-future-of-games-epic-games-tim -sweeney-fortnite-unreal-tournament.

Montag, Ali. "How This 26-Year-Old Went from Working at a Fast Food Joint to Making $500,000 a Month Playing Video Games." CNBC, March 20, 2018. https://www.cnbc.com/2018/03/20/tyler -ninja-blevins-from-working-at-noodles-co-to-twitch-gamer.html.

Statt, Nick. "Fortnite's Celebrity Tournament Felt Like a Trial Run for Epic's Grand E-sports Ambitions." Verge, June 17, 2018. https://

www.theverge.com/2018/6/17/17471216/fortnite-pro-am
-tournament-epic-games-e-sports-celebrity-e3-2018.

Tassi, Paul. "'Fortnite' Legend Ninja Talks Twitch Fame and
Fortune, and the Game That Got Him There." *Forbes*, March 13,
2018. https://www.forbes.com/sites/insertcoin/2018/03/13
/fortnite-legend-ninja-talks-twitch-fame-and-fortune-and-the
-game-that-got-him-there.

TooFab Staff. "'Fortnite' Gamer Ninja on How He Got His Name and
Why the Game Is Such a Hit." Toofab.com, July 25, 2018. http://
toofab.com/2018/07/23/fortnite-gamer-ninja-on-how-he-got-his
-name-and-why-the-game-is-such-a-hit.

Tsukayama, Hayley. "Everything You Need to Know about Fortnite
and Why It's So Popular." *Washington Post*, April 3, 2018.
https://www.washingtonpost.com/news/the-switch
/wp/2018/04/03/everything-you-need-to-know-about-fortnite
-and-why-its-so-popular/?utm_term=.11d31b0ba5e3.

Twitch.tv. "Frequently Asked Questions." Twitch.tv, Retrieved
December 3, 2018. https://www.twitch.tv/p/partners/faq.

Valens, Ana. "Report Shows Twitch Audience Bigger than HBO's
and Netflix's." Dotesports.com, October 18, 2017. https://
dotesports.com/the-op/news/twitch-audience-hbo-netflix-18122.

Walshy. "Walshy's Halo History: Episode 5—Featuring Ninja from
Team Liquid." YouTube.com, May 20, 2015. https://
www.youtube.com/watch?v=_IP1K9UF7js.

Warman, Peter. "Esports revenues will reach $696 million this year
and grow to $1.5 billion by 2020 as brand investment doubles."
Newzoo.com, February 14, 2017. https://newzoo.com/insights
/articles/esports-revenues-will-reach-696-million-in-2017.

INDEX

About the Author

Adam Furgang has been writing books for middle-grade readers for more than a decade. He was fortunate enough to be raised in the 1970s, the golden age of gaming. He was among the first generation of kids to play video games at home. He has more than three decades of experience playing video games, Dungeons & Dragons, and numerous tabletop role-playing and board games. He continues to play games of all types with his two sons, one of whom is a huge fan of Ninja and *Fortnite*. He also runs a blog, wizardsneverweararmor.com, that concentrates on gaming, art, and films.

Photo Credits

Cover, pp. 5, 22, 25, 32 Ethan Miller/Getty Images; p. 8 James Leynse/Corbis Historical/Getty Images; p. 10 Barone Firenze/Shutterstock.com; pp. 11, 16 ZUMA Press, Inc./Alamy Stock Photo; pp. 14–15 Jeff Vinnick/Getty Images; p. 18 Michael Moloney/Shutterstock.com; p. 20 The Washington Post/Getty Images; p. 26 360b/Shutterstock.com; p. 29 Sundry Photography/Shutterstock.com; p. 33 Bloomberg/Getty Images; p. 34 Kevin Mazur/Getty Images; p. 36 Edge Magazine/Future/Getty Images; cover, p. 1 triangle pattern Maxger/Shutterstock.com; cover vertical pattern chanchai howharn/Shutterstock.com; back cover pattern Onchira Wongsiri/Shutterstock.com; interior pages hexagon pattern Ink Drop/Shutterstock.com; interior pages additional geometric pattern Iuzvykova Iaroslava/Shutterstock.com.

Design and Layout: Brian Garvey; Editor: Siyavush Saidian; Photo Researcher: Nicole DiMella